GW00361093

Belinda Jeffery's

salad
perfection
COOKING CLASS

All rights of the producer and of the recorded work reserved. Unauthorised copying, hiring, lending, public performance and broadcasting of this recording prohibited.

salad *perfection*

HINKLER BOOKS

salad
perfection

Food Editor
Ellen Argyriou

Creative Director
Sam Grimmer

Project Editor
Lara Morcombe

HINKLER
BOOKS

First published in 2004 by Hinkler Books Pty Ltd
17–23 Redwood Drive
Dingley, VIC 3172 Australia
www.hinklerbooks.com

Printed in 2004

© Text and Design Hinkler Books Pty Ltd
© Step-by-Step Shots and Hero Shots on pages 16, 23, 33, 37, 40, 49, 50, 51,
52, 55, 56, 62, 63, 69, 70-71, 73 Hinkler Books Pty Ltd
© Hero Shots on pages 12, 13, 14-15, 17, 18, 19, 20-21, 22, 26, 27, 28, 29,
30-31, 32, 34-35, 36, 38-39, 41, 44, 45, 46, 47, 48, 53, 54, 57, 60-61, 64-65, 66, 67, 68, 72
R&R Publications licensed to Hinkler Books Pty Ltd

All rights reserved. No part of this publication may be reproduced, stored in a retrieval system, or transmitted in any
way or by any means, electronic, mechanical, photocopying, recording or otherwise, without the prior written
permission of Hinkler Books Pty Ltd.
Disclaimer: The nutritional information listed under each recipe does not include the nutrient content of garnishes or
any accompaniments not listed in specific quantitites in the ingredient list. The nutritional information for each recipe
is an estimate only, and may vary depending on the brand of ingredients used, and due to natural biological variations
in the composition of natural foods such as meat, fish, fruit and vegetables. The nutritional information was calculated
by using Foodworks dietary analysis software (Version 3, Xyris Software Pty Ltd, Highgate Hill, Queensland, Australia)
based on the Australian food composition tables and food manufacturers' data. Where not specified, ingredients are
always analyzed as average or medium, not small or large.

ISBN: 1 7412 1595 1
EAN: 9781741215953

Printed and bound in China

contents

an introduction to salads

Crisp, refreshing, colorful, delicious, light, appealing, wholesome and healthy are all the words that come to mind when we think of salads. They are nature's gift to our health status and to our meal table.

The value of salads in our diet cannot be underestimated. They provide, first and foremost, valuable nutrients such as vitamins and minerals, which are not lost through cooking. They add variety and interest to our diet, color to our table and elevate the most simple meal.

Salad ingredients were once restricted to the traditional varieties of the various cuisines around the world. Today, with the interchange of ethnic cuisines the demand for new salad produce has crossed continents and climatic zones and everything is available to all. We can all enjoy salad combinations outside our own traditional fare. We can combine the fruits of the tropics with the vegetables of the temperate zones, the flavors of the west with the more exotic flavors of the east. This book explores this amazing interchange.

Although divided into chapters featuring salads for appetizers, entrées, side salads and salads to serve at a buffet when entertaining, any salad recipe can be used for any occasion. An appetizer salad for 4 can be doubled to become a buffet salad for 8–10 and a buffet salad can be halved to become a main meal salad.

Salads are not only for summer meals, they can and should be served all the year.

The following salad greens are known by several names. This pictorial guide will assist you to identify the ingredient you require.

cos lettuce
Has a crisp leaf and a sweetish nutty flavor. Known as: cos, romaine.

iceberg lettuce
Crisp leaves packed tightly into a round head. Known as: iceberg lettuce, crisphead lettuce.

mignonette lettuce
Soft tender leaves tinged with red. Known as: mignonette lettuce, cabbage lettuce.

green and red coral lettuce
Green or red frilled leaves. Do not form a heart. Known as: green coral or red coral, loose-leaf lettuce.

butter lettuce
Tender soft leaf lettuce with buttery flavor. Known as: butter lettuce, butterhead.

endive
Crisp leaf with a slight bitter flavor. Known as: endive, chicory, curly endive.

rocket
A flavorsome leaf with a mustard tang. Known as: rocket, roquette, arugula.

radicchio
A beautiful ruby color with thick white veins; a very attractive leaf for presentation. Known as: radicchio, red leaved chicory, italian chicory, italian red lettuce.

witlof
Crisp white leaves with a sharp mild bitter flavor. Known as: witlof, belgian endive, french endive, witloof chicory.

green onions
A young bulb onion harvested before the bulb has formed. With a mild flavor and crisp texture, it is in great demand for salads. Known as: fresh green onions, spring onions, scallions, welsh onions, bunching onions.

spanish onions
Red in color, these onions have a mild sweetish flavor. There are many varieties. Known as: spanish onion, italian red onion.

flat-leaf parsley
Parsley with a flat leaf and a more intense flavor than the curly parsley. Known as: flat-leaf parsley, continental parsley.

salad tips and skills

Salad greens and other salad vegetables must be stored correctly to retain freshness and quality. Do not wash any vegetables before storing. Greens that are tied in bunches such as spinach, endive and rocket should be opened out and checked. If damp in the center, pat dry before storing.

Salad greens should be stored in the vegetable compartment of the refrigerator. As the level of vegetables in the compartment lowers, place a clean dishtowel lightly over their surface to prevent moisture being drawn from them to fill the space. Have you ever wondered why the last few pieces in the vegetable compartment have wilted?

If there is no room in the vegetable container, salad vegetables may be placed on the lower shelves in a plastic bag, covered plastic container or on a tray covered with a clean cloth or plastic wrap. The important point is to cover their surface to prevent moisture loss.

Root vegetables may be stored on a rack in a well ventilated dark place.

All vegetables and fruits must be washed well before peeling and cutting.

Salad greens must be washed well in 2–3 changes of water to remove all grit, or in a colander under trickling cold water, not to bruise the tender leaves. Drain well.

Root vegetables need to be scrubbed with a brush under running water to remove all dirt, particularly if being cooked with the skin on.

For a good salad, leaves need to be dried well before placing in the bowl. The dressing will not adhere to wet leaves and the excess moisture will dilute the dressing. A salad spinner is excellent. It will spin all the water off. You may pat dry the leaves with absorbent paper or shake dry in a clean dishtowel.

To crisp the salad leaves roll up in a damp cloth and refrigerate for 1 hour or until you are ready to serve.

deseeding tomatoes
Cut the tomato in half across the center. Cup the tomato in your hand and squeeze out the seeds.

to trim asparagus
Using a potato peeler or sharp paring knife peel off the thicker skin on the lower part of the stalk.

to segment an orange or grapefruit
1 Peel the orange or grapefruit thickly, removing all the white pith.

2 Holding the orange or grapefruit over a bowl to catch the juice, cut close to the membrane on each side of the segment and ease the segment out. Continue to the next segment.

to deseed a cucumber
Cut the cucumber in half lengthwise. Run the point of a teaspoon down the seeds, pressing inwards to remove the seeds.

to toast nuts

1 Place nuts in a shallow baking pan and place in a moderate oven 180°C (350°F, gas mark 4) for 10 minutes or until golden. The nuts will crisp on cooling. A deep coloration will impart a bitter flavor.

2 Heat a heavy-bottomed skillet until hot. Add the nuts and stir with a wooden spoon until they color. Remove from the pan immediately desired color is attained.

to blanch almonds

Place in a bowl and cover with hot water. Stand for 10 minutes then slip off skins.

to peel bell pepper

Trim the top and base of each pepper and cut into quarters making 4 flat pieces. Trim off any inside veins and rub skin side with oil. Place skin side up, under a preheated hot broiler and cook until skins are blistered. Place in a plastic bag closing the end and set aside until cool enough to handle. With the aid of a small knife lift the edge of the skin and peel off.

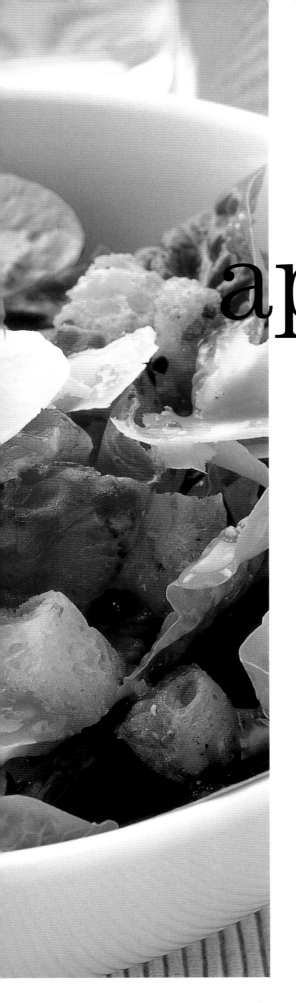

appetizers

watercress and pear salad

ingredients

2 bunches watercress, plucked and
washed
3 tablespoons olive oil
1 tablespoon lemon juice
$1/2$ tablespoon white-wine vinegar
salt and pepper
3 beurre bosc pears, washed
parmesan shavings

serves 6–8

i

preparation time
8 minutes

**nutritional value
per serve**
fat: 5.6 g
carbohydrate: 6.4 g
protein: 2.1 g

1 Slice pears finely and combine with watercress in a bowl.

2 Beat oil, lemon juice and white-wine vinegar with salt and pepper until slightly thickened. Drizzle over salad just enough to coat the leaves. Place on a platter and top with shavings of parmesan.

witlof salad with pecans

ingredients

5 heads witlof (belgian endive), washed
1 red delicious apple, quartered
1 green apple, quartered
juice of 1 lemon
200 g (7 oz) young rocket leaves
160 g (5½ oz) pecan nuts, coarsely
  chopped and toasted
100 g (3½ oz) gorgonzola or blue
  castello, crumbled

dressing

4 tablespoons olive oil
4 tablespoons walnut oil
4 tablespoons sherry-wine vinegar
1 large green onion, finely chopped
salt and pepper

serves 6

i

preparation time
15 minutes

nutritional value
per serve
fat: 8.2 g
carbohydrate: 1.9 g
protein: 2.3 g

1 Cut the witlof in half, lengthwise then lay the witlof cut side down on a board and cut the leaves into thin strips.

2 Toss apples with the lemon juice. Wash the rocket leaves and drain well.

3 In a bowl, combine witlof, apple slices, rocket, toasted

pecans and blue cheese. Beat together walnut and olive oil, sherry-wine vinegar and green onion, and salt and pepper to taste. Drizzle over the salad and toss. Serve immediately.

favorite caesar salad

ingredients

5 cloves garlic, minced
4 tablespoons olive oil
9 slices anchovies
juice of 1¹/₂ lemons
2 teaspoons worcestershire sauce
1 teaspoon mustard
1 ¹/₂ tablepoons white-wine vinegar
4 eggs
2 thick slices country-style bread
2 tablespoons olive oil
100 g (3¹/₂ oz) prosciutto
3 heads cos lettuce, washed and crisped
50 g (1 ³/₄ oz) parmesan
salt
freshly ground black pepper
serves 6-8

preparation time
15 minutes

cooking time
15 minutes

nutritional value per serve
fat: 9.5 g
carbohydrate: 2.8 g
protein: 5.1 g

1 Preheat the oven to 220°C (430°F, gas mark 7). Cut the bread into cubes and toss with the olive oil and salt and pepper. Transfer to a baking pan and bake the cubes for 15 minutes until golden and cool. Crisp the prosciutto on a shallow pan in the oven for 3 minutes.

2 In a large mixing bowl, place garlic and olive oil, using the back of a metal spoon, press the garlic into the oil. Add the anchovies and mash into the oil mixture. Beat in lemon juice, worcestershire sauce, mustard and white-wine vinegar, mixing each ingredient thoroughly before the next is added.

3 Boil the eggs for 1 minute. Remove immediately and allow to cool. Crack the egg carefully, separate the yolks and mix well into the ingredients in the bowl.

4 Place lettuce leaves in a mixing bowl and toss thoroughly in the dressing for several minutes until all leaves are coated. Add bread cubes, parmesan, and finish with black pepper and crisp prosciutto. Serve immediately.

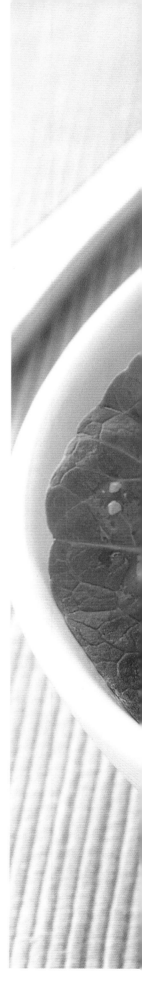

1 Arrange apple wedges in a salad bowl and sprinkle with 1 tablespoon vinaigrette.

2 Wash watercress, drain well and pat dry in a dishtowel. Break the watercress into small sprigs discarding coarse stems. Add to apples, with onion and chives.

3 Crumble cheese over salad. Drizzle remaining dressing over top.

apple and watercress salad with blue cheese

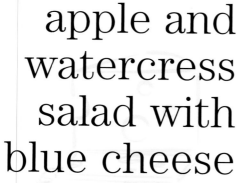

ingredients

2 green apples, cut into wedges
4 tablespoons vinaigrette
1 bunch watercress
½ spanish onion, sliced
3 tablespoons chives, finely chopped
155 g (5 oz) blue-veined cheese
serves 6

i

preparation time
15 minutes

**nutritional value
per serve**
fat: 7.6 g
carbohydrate: 7.1 g
protein: 5.2 g

jumbo shrimp with mango salsa

ingredients

12 raw jumbo shrimp, peeled (tails on)
flour seasoned with salt and pepper
   for dusting
1 egg, beaten
155 g (5 oz) sesame seeds
90 g (3 oz) shredded coconut
1 mango, peeled and finely diced
1/2 small spanish onion, finely diced
2 tablespoons cilantro
juice of 1 lime
2 tablespoons butter or olive oil
150 g (5 oz) mixed salad greens
   of your choice
lime quarters for garnish
serves 4

1 Butterfly the shrimp, cutting along the inner curve, 3/4 of the way through and to the vein. Open out, remove the vein and flatten by pressing down with side of a large knife.

2 Dip each shrimp into the seasoned flour then into the beaten egg to coat both sides.

Place onto the coconut mixture, covering the top also, and pressing down lightly for the mixture to adhere. Place the shrimp on a flat oven sheet and refrigerate 20 minutes or more.

3 In a skillet, heat the butter or olive oil, add shrimp and

fry over a high heat for 1–2 minutes each side until golden. (You may need to apply pressure with a spatula as they cook to prevent them from curling up.)

4 Combine mango, onion, cilantro and lime juice in a bowl and add salt and pepper to taste. To serve, arrange some salad greens on each plate and top with 3 cooked shrimp and a generous spoonful of the mango salsa. Drizzle over any remaining salsa juice and serve immediately with lime wedges if desired.

preparation time
15 minutes,
plus 20 minutes
refrigeration

cooking time
3 minutes

**nutritional value
per serve**
fat: 17.3 g
carbohydrate: 3.7 g
protein: 9.4 g

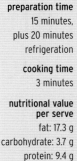

rock lobster and smoked ocean trout salad

ingredients

2 lobster tails, cooked
400 g (13 oz) smoked ocean trout
1 continental cucumber
1 carrot
1 green small zucchini
1 yellow small zucchini
100 g (3½ oz) rocket leaves
1 bunch chives, finely chopped

dressing
juice of 2 limes
1 tablespoon palm sugar or light brown
  sugar
½ cup (125 ml, 4 fl oz) olive oil
salt and pepper

serves 6

1 Remove the meat from the lobster tails and slice finely. Cut trout into thin strips. Place lobster and trout in a container, cover and refrigerate.

i

preparation time
20 minutes

**nutritional value
per serve**
fat: 9.8 g
carbohydrate: 1.9 g
protein: 11 g

2 Wash the cucumber, slice in half lengthways, scoop out and discard the seeds. Using a potato peeler or vegetable slicer, cut the cucumber and carrot into long thin ribbons. Cut the unpeeled green and yellow zucchini into long thin ribbons. Mix the lobster, ocean trout, ribboned vegetables and rocket leaves gently together in a large bowl.

3 In a bowl, place the lime juice and palm sugar. Heat in the microwave or over hot water to dissolve the sugar. Beat in the olive oil, add the salt and pepper and beat until it thickens. Toss gently through the salad. Arrange the salad on an attractive platter and sprinkle over chives.

broiled goat cheese salad

ingredients

4 small fresh goat cheeses
2 sprigs fresh thyme
1 clove garlic, minced
⅓ cup (80 ml, 2 ³/₄ fl oz) extra virgin
  olive oil
cracked black pepper
4 thin lemon slices, halved
300 g (10 oz) mixed salad leaves,
  washed and crisped
slices of country-style bread, toasted
serves 4

1 Place the cheese in a container that will fit them neatly. Strip the thyme leaves from the stalk into a bowl. Add garlic, oil and cracked pepper and mix well. Pour over the cheeses and

place lemon slices between the cheeses. Cover and marinate in the refrigerator for 4–6 hours. Turn cheeses in the marinade once or twice.

2 Preheat the broiler. Broil the cheese for 2 minutes each side and the lemon slices until rosy tinged and softened a little.

3 Arrange salad leaves on 4 plates. Place a cheese and lemon slice on each and drizzle with marinade. Toast the bread and serve with the salad.

i

preparation time
10 minutes

marinating time
4-6 hours

**nutritional value
per serve**
fat: 18.3 g
carbohydrate: 1.1 g
protein: 3.5 g

armenian stuffed tomato salad

ingredients

8 large, round tomatoes
4 tablespoons olive oil
1 large onion, finely chopped
1 large leek, finely chopped
3 cups (555 g, 1 lb) steamed or boiled
   white or brown rice
80 g (2³/₄ oz) pine nuts, toasted
110 g (3¹/₂ oz) currants
1 handful parsley, chopped
1 tablespoon chopped fresh mint
³/₄ teaspoon sea salt
¹/₂ teaspoon black pepper
2 cloves garlic, minced
¹/₂ cup (125 ml, 4 fl oz) vegetable stock
¹/₂ cup (125 ml, 4 fl oz) white wine
500 g (1 lb) baby spinach leaves,
   washed and drained

serves 8

3 Fill each tomato with the rice mixture and replace the tops of the tomatoes. Place in a baking pan. Combine garlic, stock and white wine and pour around tomatoes. Bake for 20 minutes. Remove from oven.

1 Preheat the oven to 180°C (350°F, gas mark 4). With a sharp knife, slice the tops off the tomatoes, scoop out as much flesh as possible without damaging the exterior of the tomato. Chop the removed flesh finely.

4 Place spinach leaves in a bowl. Spoon some of the hot cooking liquid from the tomatoes over the spinach, discard the garlic, and toss well. Serve a mound of warm spinach on each plate with the tomato placed on top. Drizzle any remaining liquid over and serve.

2 Heat the oil in a skillet and cook onion and leek until slightly golden. Add rice, tomato pulp, nuts, currants, parsley, mint, salt and pepper and sauté until the mixture is hot and well flavored.

preparation time
20 minutes

cooking time
20 minutes

**nutritional value
per serve**
fat: 4.3 g
carbohydrate: 8.1 g
protein: 1.8 g

carrot and shrimp tapas salad

ingredients

750 g (1½ lb) carrots, peeled and
  diagonally sliced
4 cloves garlic, very finely chopped
1 tablespoon finely chopped fresh
  rosemary
3 tablespoons virgin olive oil
1 teaspoon ground cumin
2 teaspoons mild paprika
2 tablespoons white-wine vinegar
salt and freshly ground black pepper
500 g (1 lb) jumbo shrimp, cooked and
  peeled (tails on)
1 handful flat-leaf parsley, chopped

serves 6

preparation time
10 minutes

cooking time
6 minutes

**nutritional value
per serve**
fat: 4.2 g
carbohydrate: 2.9 g
protein: 7.1 g

1 Place carrots in a pan of boiling water and boil vigorously for 3–4 minutes until almost crisp-tender. Drain.

2 Heat a tablespoon of oil in a small skillet and add garlic, rosemary, cumin and paprika. Sauté for 1–2 minutes until fragrant. Remove from the heat and beat in remaining olive oil and white-wine vinegar. Add salt and pepper to taste.

3 Toss the carrot slices and cooked shrimp with the warm garlic rosemary dressing to coat well. Place in a dish and garnish with fresh parsley leaves.

melon and onion salad

ingredients

$1/2$ (about 1 kg, 2 lb) medium seedless
   watermelon
2 medium-sized red onions,
   thinly sliced
dressing
4 tablespoons lemon juice
1 tablespoon honey
5 tablespoons salad oil
salt
freshly ground black pepper
serves 6-8

1 Slice watermelon thinly,
discarding seeds. Using a
pastry cutter, cut slices into
rounds, about same size as
largest onion rings in
concentric circles in a large
oval pan or entrée plate.

2 Place lemon juice, honey,
salad oil, salt and pepper in
a bowl. Beat. Pour dressing
over salad, cover and marinate
in refrigerator overnight.
Served chilled.

preparation time
15 minutes

**nutritional value
per serve**
fat: 6.7 g
carbohydrate: 6.2 g
protein: 0.4 g

entrées

asian chicken bok choy salad

ingredients

8 fresh or dried shiitake mushrooms
10 g (1/3 oz) black cloud fungus
800 g (1 lb 10 oz) cooked chicken, skin off and shredded
1 kg (2 lb) fresh asian hokkien noodles
200 g (7 oz) fresh sugar snap peas, diagonally sliced
4 bok choy (pak choi), washed and leaves separated
1 red bell pepper, diced
4 green onions, finely sliced
250 g (8 oz) can sliced water chestnuts, drained
1 tablespoon finely chopped ginger
4 tablespoons plain low-fat yogurt
3 tablespoons kecap manis
1 tablespoon hoisin sauce
3 tablespoons mirin
3 tablespoons rice vinegar
3 tablespoons sweet chilli sauce
1 tablespoon fish sauce
juice of 1 lime
2 tablespoons slivered almonds, toasted
1 bunch chervil, parsley or cilantro
salt and pepper

serves 4–6

i

preparation time
20 minutes

**nutritional value
per serve**
fat: 4 g
carbohydrate: 8.4 g
protein: 7.8 g

1 Slice the fresh shiitake mushrooms finely or soak dried shiitake mushrooms in hot water for 15 minutes, rinse in cold water, drain and slice finely. Soak the black cloud fungus for 15 minutes then drain.

2 Place the chicken in a large bowl. Separate the cooked noodles under hot running water, drain well and add to the chicken. Add the mushrooms, sugar snap peas, bok choy, bell pepper, green onions and water chestnuts, toss well.

3 In a pitcher, beat together the ginger, yogurt, kecap manis, hoisin, mirin, rice vinegar, sweet chilli sauce, fish sauce, lime juice, and salt and pepper to taste. Add to the chicken salad and toss until all ingredients are coated well. Garnish with almonds and chervil, parsley or cilantro.

bean and chickpea salad with artichokes and hazelnuts

ingredients

600 g (1¼ lb) green beans
2 x 240 g (8 oz) can chickpeas
8 preserved artichoke hearts, quartered
1 small spanish onion, finely sliced
1 medium carrot, grated
2 handfuls parsley, chopped
2 handfuls cilantro, chopped
2 tablespoons fresh dill
2 tablespoons white-wine vinegar
3 tablespoons olive oil
1 clove garlic, minced
1 teaspoon mustard
1 teaspoon ground cumin
juice of 1 lemon
salt and pepper
90 g (3 oz) hazelnuts, toasted and
   roughly chopped
serves 6

1 Trim the beans and cut diagonally in half. Steam, boil or microwave until bright green and crisp-tender (do not overcook), drain well and refresh in cold water.

2 In a large bowl, place beans and add artichoke hearts, rinsed chickpeas, spanish onion, carrot, parsley, cilantro and dill. Stir to combine thoroughly.

3 In a pitcher, beat the vinegar, olive oil, garlic, mustard, cumin, lemon juice and salt and pepper. When emulsified (thick) pour over the vegetable mixture and toss well to coat. Sprinkle with toasted hazelnuts and serve.

i

preparation time
10 minutes

cooking time
10 minutes

**nutritional value
per serve**
fat: 6.7 g
carbohydrate: 5.8 g
protein: 3.9 g

gingered almond broccoli salad with cellophane noodles

ingredients

noodles
100 g (3¹/₂ oz) dried cellophane noodles
2 handfuls cilantro, chopped
2 tablespoons fish sauce
2 tablespoons rice vinegar
2 tablespoons mirin
1 teaspoon palm or light brown sugar

salad
1 tablespoon peanut oil
1 tablespoon grated fresh ginger
1 small hot red chilli pepper, very finely
   sliced
4 cloves garlic, finely chopped
4 green onions, finely chopped
500 g (1 lb) broccoli florets, trimmed
120 g (4 oz) blanched almonds, toasted
200 g (7 oz) can baby corn
10 fresh shiitake mushrooms, sliced
3 tablespoons soy sauce
3 tablespoons mirin
2 tablespoons rice vinegar
1 cos lettuce, shredded
extra cilantro to serve

serves 4

1 Place noodles in a bowl, cover with hot water and stand for 10 minutes until soft and tender. Drain well. In a bowl, combine the fish sauce, rice vinegar, sugar and 2 tablespoons of mirin. Toss through the cellophane noodles. Add the cilantro, mix well and set aside.

i

preparation tme
15 minutes

cooking time
5 minutes

nutritional value
per serve
fat: 4.9 g
carbohydrate: 5 g
protein: 3.8 g

2 Heat the oil in a wok and add ginger, chilli pepper, garlic and green onions. Toss thoroughly and cook for about 3 minutes. Add the broccoli florets and stir-fry until bright green. Add mushrooms and corn and stir-fry for a further 30 seconds. Add soy, rice vinegar and remaining mirin, and continue cooking for 1 minute.

3 Add the prepared noodles to the wok and mix well. Remove the wok from the heat. Divide the lettuce among the plates then top with broccoli noodle salad. Garnish with almonds and cilantro.

warm lima bean and prosciutto salad with rocket

ingredients

420 g (14 oz) can lima beans
2 tablespoons olive oil
1/2 teaspoon dried chilli flakes
3 cloves garlic, finely chopped
100 g (3 1/2 oz) prosciutto,
  roughly chopped
juice of 1 lemon
10 basil leaves, torn
1 bunch of rocket leaves
salt and freshly ground black pepper
serves 6

i

preparation time
15 minutes

cooking time
5 minutes

**nutritional value
per serve**
fat: 3 g
carbohydrate: 6.2 g
protein: 4.9 g

1 Drain the canned beans in a strainer and rinse through with cold water.

2 Heat oil in a large skillet. Add chilli flakes and garlic and sauté briefly until garlic is golden. Add prosciutto and for about 2 minutes stir over moderate heat until beginning to brown. Add lima beans and cook for 3 minutes, while tossing occasionally and adding lemon juice. Remove from heat.

3 Add basil leaves and rocket, and season with salt and pepper. Toss gently then transfer to a platter. Serve warm.

couscous salad with seafood and fresh mint

ingredients

¹/₂ cup (125 ml, 4 fl oz) olive oil
2 tablespoons lemon juice
1 large clove garlic, finely chopped
1 teaspoon celery seed
¹/₄ teaspoon turmeric
¹/₄ teaspoon cumin
1²/₃ cups (410 ml, 13 fl oz) vegetable stock
500 g (1 lb) raw jumbo shrimp, peeled (tails on)
200 g (7 oz) small calamari (squid) rings
300 g (10 oz) couscous
3 tomatoes, finely diced
2 stalks celery, finely sliced
6 green onions, chopped
20 fresh mint leaves, finely sliced
salt and pepper

serves 6

1 Beat together oil, lemon juice, garlic and celery seed until thick then season with salt and pepper. Set aside to develop flavor. In a pan, bring stock to the boil and add turmeric and cumin. Add shrimp and calamari and poach gently for 2 minutes until the shrimp are orange. Remove seafood from stock with a slotted spoon.

2 In a large bowl, place the couscous and pour over hot stock. Stir well and cover. Allow to stand for about 10 minutes until water is absorbed.

3 Toss couscous with a fork to fluff then add seafood. Toss in the diced tomatoes, celery, green onions and some of the shredded mint leaves.

4 Add the dressing and mix well then garnish with remaining mint leaves.

i

preparation time
20 minutes

cooking time
5 minutes

nutritional value per serve
fat: 5.4 g
carbohydrate: 2.1 g
protein: 6.7 g

tuscan tomato and bean salad

ingredients

12 sun-dried tomato halves
1 cup (250 ml, 8 fl oz) boiling water
1/3 cup (80 ml, 2 3/4 fl oz) rice vinegar
1 tablespoon olive oil
2 teaspoons honey
salt and pepper to taste
150 g (5 oz) baby rocket leaves
150 g (5 oz) watercress
8 roma tomatoes, diced
6 fresh green onions, sliced
80 g (2 3/4 oz) kalamata olives, pitted
2 x 440 g (14 oz) cans cannellini beans,
  rinsed and drained
100 g (3 1/2 oz) toasted walnuts, chopped
serves 4-6

i

preparation time
15 minutes

**nutritional value
per serve**
fat: 3.4 g
carbohydrate: 7.1 g
protein: 3.9 g

1 Soak the sun dried tomatoes in the boiling water until water cools. Add the rice vinegar, oil, honey and purée in a food processor until smooth. Add salt and pepper to taste.

2 Pluck the watercress sprigs from the coarse stems, and thoroughly wash with the rocket. Drain well and shake dry in a clean dishtowel. Place in a large mixing bowl and add the diced tomatoes, green onions, olives and cannellini beans.

3 Pour over the sun-dried tomato dressing and toss well to coat. Serve immediately garnished with the toasted walnuts.

herbed seafood salad

ingredients

24 poached scallops

24 jumbo shrimp, peeled, de-veined and cooked

4 tablespoons vinegar

4 tablespoons lime juice

3 tablespoons orange juice

1 clove garlic, lightly minced

1 red chilli pepper, deseeded and finely sliced

1/4 green bell pepper, cut into fine strips

60 g (2 oz) stuffed green olives, halved

2 tablespoons chopped fresh cilantro

1/2 cup (125 ml, 4 fl oz) light olive oil

lemon slices and dandelion leaves for serving

serves 8

1 Place scallops in a saucepan with just enough hot water to cover. Bring to a slow simmer and simmer for 2 minutes. Allow to cool in the liquid. In a bowl, combine scallops and shrimp. Add vinegar, lime and orange juice and garlic. Mix well, cover and chill for 2 hours.

2 Strain seafood mixture, reserving marinade. In a salad bowl, place seafood and add chilli pepper, green bell pepper, olives and cilantro. Toss. Add oil to reserved marinade and beat well. Pour dressing over salad and toss lightly. Place a few dandelion leaves on each plate. Pile the salad in the center and garnish with lemon.

preparation time
10 minutes, plus 2 hours refrigeration

cooking time
4 minutes

nutritional value per serve
fat: 10.4 g
carbohydrate: 0.7 g
protein: 13.7 g

tuna barley niçoise

ingredients

2 pink skinned potatoes, unpeeled
1 teaspoon olive oil
sea salt and pepper
2 teaspoons fresh rosemary
1 litre (1²/₃ pints) vegetable stock
1 teaspoon fresh oregano
1 teaspoon fresh marjoram
220 g (7¹/₂ oz) pearl barley
1 spanish onion, finely sliced
6 tuna steaks
500 g (1 lb) green beans, blanched
2 handfuls fresh parsley, chopped
90 g (3 oz) baby lettuce leaves
   (mesclun)
2 hard boiled eggs, sliced
2 red bell peppers, roasted
2 roma tomatoes, finely chopped
140 g (4¹/₂ oz) kalamata olives,
   finely chopped

dressing

juice of 3 lemons
juice of 1 lime
1 tablespoon red-wine vinegar
2 tablespoons anchovy paste
4 cloves garlic, minced
1 teaspoon mixed dried herbs
1-2 tablespoons virgin olive oil
1 teaspoon dijon mustard
¹/₂ cup (125 ml, 4 fl oz) vegetable stock

serves 6

i

preparation time
35 minutes, plus
30 minutes
soaking

cooking time
1 hour 25 minutes

**nutritional value
per serve**
fat: 2.6 g
carbohydrate: 5.6 g
protein: 7.5 g

1 Preheat oven to 220°C (425°F, gas mark 7). Slice the potatoes into ¹/₄ inch slices. Brush with olive oil and sprinkle with sea salt, pepper and rosemary. Place in a baking pan and cook for 45 minutes, turning once.

2 Bring stock to the boil, add oregano, marjoram and barley, cover and simmer for 40 minutes. Remove from heat and set aside. Soak spanish onion in cold water for 30 minutes, then drain.

3 Season tuna steaks with salt and pepper and cook on a preheated broiler pan for 2 minutes each side, until just cooked, or alternatively bake at 210°C (415°F, gas mark 6–7) for 7 minutes.

4 Beat together lemon and lime juice, vinegar, anchovy paste, garlic, dried herbs, dijon mustard, ¹/₂ cup of stock and virgin olive oil until thick then set aside. Mix green beans, onions rings, parsley and half the dressing with the warm barley and toss thoroughly to distribute.

5 To assemble, place several slices of potato on the center of each plate, top with a few lettuce leaves, a generous spoonful of barley mixture, some egg slices, some roasted bell pepper and a cooked fillet of tuna. Place teaspoonfuls of tomato and olives around the salad, then drizzle everything with remaining dressing. Sprinkle with remaining parsley and serve immediately.

summer salad of broiled chicken, spinach and mango

ingredients

salad

6 roma tomatoes
10 basil leaves, chopped
10 mint leaves, chopped
salt and black pepper
1/2 teaspoon sugar
12 chicken tenderloins (from breasts)
1 bunch of asparagus, trimmed and
  steamed
1 avocado, diced
1 bunch green onions, diagonally sliced
8 firm button mushrooms, sliced
2 firm mangoes, peeled and cut into dice
150 g (5 oz) baby spinach leaves
60 g (2 oz) toasted hazelnuts,
  lightly crushed
60 g (2 oz) toasted brazil nuts,
  lightly crushed
60 g (2 oz) toasted pistachio nuts,
  lightly crushed

dressing

2 teaspoons honey
2 tablespoons balsamic vinegar
3 tablespoons raspberry vinegar
2 teaspoons dijon mustard
2 teaspoons finely chopped ginger
2 cloves garlic, minced
2 tablespoons lemon juice
2 tablespoons olive oil
salt and freshly ground black pepper

serves 6

i

preparation time
30 minutes, plus
2 hours
refrigeration

cooking time
2 hours

**nutritional value
per serve**
fat: 7.5 g
carbohydrate: 3 g
protein: 8 g

1 Preheat oven 160°C (315°F, gas mark 2–3). Slice the tomatoes in half lengthways, and top with basil, mint, salt, pepper and sugar. Bake for 2 hours. When cooked and cool, slice each half in two.

2 Beat together honey, vinegars, dijon mustard, ginger, garlic, lemon juice, olive oil and salt and pepper until thick. Place chicken tenderloins in a container, pour over 1/2 the dressing. Cover and allow to marinate for 2 hours or more in the refrigerator. Heat a non-stick broiler pan and cook the chicken fillets over a high heat for 2–3 minutes on each side until cooked through. Transfer fillets to a plate and keep warm.

3 In a large bowl, place spinach leaves and add asparagus, green onions, mushrooms and roasted tomatoes. Add remaining dressing and toss thoroughly.

4 Divide the salad evenly among individual plates and add some mango and avocado cubes. Top with 2 fillets of chicken, and a generous sprinkling of nuts. Serve immediately.

potato and smoked sausage salad

2 Heat remaining oil in a skillet. Add asparagus and green onions and stir-fry for 2 minutes. Transfer vegetables to a bowl. Add roast potatoes.

3 Thinly slice the hot sausage and add to vegetables in bowl. Toss mixture lightly and arrange on a serving plate. Blend chives with garlic, lemon juice, yogurt and sour cream until smooth. Pour over salad, garnish with whole chives and serve.

ingredients

500 g (1 lb) small chat potatoes
4 tablespoons oil
1 teaspoon salt
2 smoked pork sausages (e.g., chorizo)
1 bunch asparagus, cut into 1 inch lengths
2 tablespoons chopped green onions
2 tablespoons chives, finely chopped
1 clove garlic, minced
2 teaspoons lemon juice
$^1/_3$ cup (90 ml, 3 fl oz) natural yogurt
$^1/_3$ cup (90 ml, 3 fl oz) sour cream
whole chives for garnish
serves 4-6

preparation time
10 minutes

cooking time
50 minutes

nutritional value per serve
fat: 14.7 g
carbohydrate: 17 g
protein: 7.7 g

1 Preheat oven to 200°C (400°F, Gas Mark 6). Cook potatoes in boiling water for 10 minutes, then drain. Toss potatoes in 2 tablespoons oil, sprinkle with salt and spread out on a shallow baking pan. Roast for 30 minutes until golden brown and crisp, turning occasionally. Heat sausages in a pan in the oven for 15 minutes.

seared tuna salad with crisp wontons

ingredients

tuna salad
2 tablespoons peanut oil
1 small red chilli pepper, deseeded and
    finely chopped
8 green onions, finely sliced diagonally
100 g (3½ oz) can baby corn
150 g (5 oz) sugar snap peas, trimmed
4 tablespoons sesame seeds
4 tablespoons nigella (black onion seeds)
4 x 150 g (5 oz) tuna steaks
salt and pepper
5 tablespoons vegetable oil
8 wonton wrappers, cut into thin strips
250 g (8 oz) mixed baby lettuce leaves
    (mesclun)

dressing
½ cup (125 ml, 4 fl oz) olive oil
4 tablespoons fresh lime juice
4 tablespoons orange juice
2 tablespoons soy sauce
2 tablespoons rice vinegar
1 tablespoon sesame oil
½ bunch fresh chives, finely chopped
1 tablespoon finely chopped fresh ginger
salt and pepper
serves 4-6

i

preparation time
30 minutes
cooking time
10 minutes
**nutritional value
per serve**
fat: 16.5 g
carbohydrate: 3.2 g
protein: 9.2 g

1 In a small bowl, beat together olive and sesame oil, lime and orange juice, soy sauce, vinegar, chives and ginger. Add salt and pepper to taste. Cover and set aside. Heat 1 tablespoon of peanut oil in a skillet or wok and add chilli pepper, green onions, baby corn and sugar snap peas, tossing over a high heat for 3 minutes until crisp tender. Transfer the vegetables to a bowl and drizzle over a little dressing. Set aside.

2 Season the fish with salt and pepper. Mix sesame seeds and nigella on a flat plate. Press the fish into the seed mixture, coating both sides evenly. Heat remaining peanut oil in the skillet. Add the tuna and sear over a high heat turning once until the fish is just cooked through. Transfer to a plate and allow to cool completely. Using a sharp knife, slice each fillet thinly.

3 To prepare the wontons, heat vegetable oil in a skillet or wok and, when very hot, add the strips of wonton and cook until golden brown. Remove from the skillet and drain on absorbent paper. Add salt to taste.

4 Toss the lettuce leaves with the cooked vegetable mixture and a little more dressing. Add salt and pepper to taste. Divide the lettuce mixture between 4 plates and top with the sliced, seared tuna slices. Arrange a bundle of fried wonton strips on top. Serve immediately.

warm steak salad with papaya and spanish onion

ingredients

750 g (1½ lb) beef tenderloin (fillet steak), trimmed
1 tablespoon finely chopped rosemary
¼ teaspoon cayenne pepper
1 tablespoon butter
2 teaspoons oil
1 small papaya, peeled, deseeded and cut into bite-size cubes
1 small spanish onion, thinly sliced
1 small bunch endive (curly chicory), torn into bite-size pieces
2 oranges, segmented

dressing
2 tablespoons red-wine vinegar
5 tablespoons olive oil
salt and freshly ground black pepper

serves 4-6

2 Sprinkle meat strips with rosemary and cayenne. Heat the butter and oil in a large heavy-bottomed skillet, add half of the meat and cook over high heat for 1–2 minutes, tossing gently. Remove to a bowl and cook remainder.

3 Mix the papaya and spanish onion into the steak strips. Add dressing and toss well.

1 Beat together vinegar, 5 tablespoons of oil, salt and pepper and set aside. Trim silver membrane from beef tenderloin. With a sharp knife thinly slice, then cut each slice into strips. To slice easily, place the meat in the freezer for 35 minutes until it begins to firm up. It will be firmer under the knife blade and will cut straight.

4 Combine together endive and orange segments. Place on a serving platter and pile the beef strips in the center. Serve immediately.

i

preparation time
20 minutes

cooking time
4 minutes

nutritional value
per serve
fat: 12.5 g
carbohydrate: 2 g
protein: 13.6 g

ocean trout with palm sugar sauce and noodle salad

ingredients

2 tablespoons olive oil
10 green onions, chopped
200 g (7 oz) palm sugar
100 ml (3^1/$_2$ fl oz) fish sauce
110 g (3^1/$_2$ oz) fresh ginger,
   cut into fine strips
10 small chilli peppers, deseeded and
   cut into fine strips
2 tablespoons lime juice
200 g (7 oz) cellophane noodles
1 bunch cilantro, chopped
500 g (1 lb) ocean trout fillets, cut into
   1 inch-wide pieces
extra cilantro, for garnish
serves 4

i

preparation time
15 minutes

cooking time
10 minutes

**nutritional value
per serve**
fat: 4.4 g
carbohydrate: 18 g
protein: 9.8 g

1 Heat the oil in a small skillet and gently sauté the green onions until golden. Add the palm sugar and heat until dissolved. Cook on a medium heat for about 5 minutes until the mixture has caramelized, stir well. Add the fish sauce, ginger, chilli peppers and lime juice. Stir well to combine. Remove from heat and cover.

2 Soak the cellophane noodles in hot water for about 10 minutes until softened, then refresh in cold water. Drain and place in a bowl. Add the cilantro and enough palm sugar sauce to moisten the noodles.

3 Fry in a skillet or broil the fish fillets for about 2 minutes each side until just cooked. Arrange the cellophane noodle salad on individual plates then place the fish pieces on top. Garnish with cilantro and spoon over more sauce.

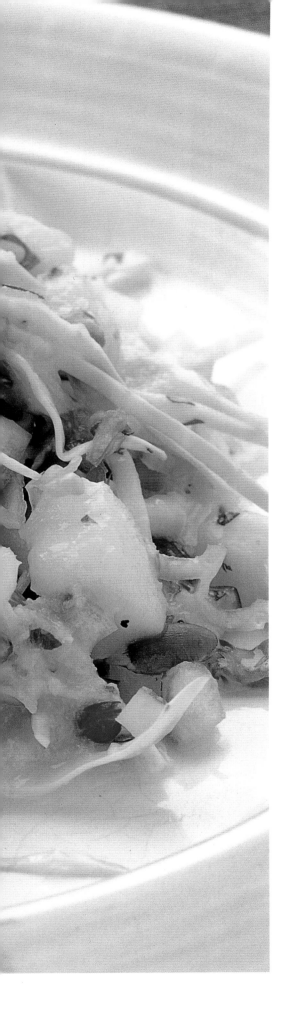

side salads

1 In a large bowl, place cabbage, green onions and cilantro. Slice bok choy widthways and add. Toss to combine.

2 Rinse, drain and then dry the chinese noodles in a clean dishtowel. Heat 1 tablespoon of oil in a skillet, add noodles and stir-fry for 2 minutes. Remove and allow to cool slightly.

3 In a salad bowl, combine the cabbage mixture, toasted nuts and fried noodles. Beat vinegar, lime or lemon juice, sugar, soy sauce and remaining oil until thick. Add salt and pepper to taste. Pour over the dressing and toss well. Serve immediately.

cabbage and chinese noodle salad

ingredients

salad

½ savoy cabbage (curly cabbage), finely shredded

4 baby bok choy (pak choi)

8 green onions, finely sliced

½ bunch cilantro, roughly chopped

90 g (3 oz) flaked almonds, toasted

70 g (2¼ oz) pine nuts, toasted

100 g (3½ oz) fresh chinese noodles

1 tablespoon peanut oil

dressing

4 tablespoons peanut oil

2 tablespoons balsamic vinegar

2 tablespoons lime or lemon juice

1 tablespoon light brown sugar

1 tablespoon soy sauce

salt and cracked pepper

serves 4-6

i

preparation time
15 minutes

cooking time
5 minutes

nutritional value per serve
fat: 13.9 g
carbohydrate: 6.8 g
protein: 3.6 g

summer greens with lime and cilantro

ingredients

salad
2 bunches asparagus, cut in half
440 g (14 oz) sugar snap peas, trimmed
220 g (7¹/₂ oz) fresh peas, shelled
¹/₂ container cherry tomatoes, halved
dressing
2 tablespoons lime juice
3 tablespoons chopped cilantro
¹/₂ cup (125 ml, 4 fl oz) extra
    virgin olive oil
1 tablespoon white-wine vinegar
serves 6

1 Trim the stem end of the asparagus with a potato peeler. Place asparagus and

sugar snap peas in a large pan of boiling water, bring back to the boil and cook for 30 seconds. Drain immediately and place into a large bowl of iced water for 30 seconds. Drain well.

2 Cook the shelled peas in boiling water for 5 minutes

until tender, drain and refresh in iced water. Drain well.

3 Combine all vegetables and cherry tomatoes. Beat together lime juice, cilantro, oil and vinegar until well combined, drizzle over vegetables, transfer to a salad platter and serve.

i

preparation time
15 minutes

cooking time
6 minutes

**nutritional value
per serve**
fat: 8.8 g
carbohydrate: 3.8 g
protein: 2.7 g

russian cabbage salad

ingredients

1 kg (2 lb) savoy cabbage (curly cabbage)
1 spanish onion
6 green onions, roughly chopped
2 cloves garlic, finely chopped
¼ teaspoon chilli flakes
4 tablespoons chopped fresh dill
4 tablespoons chopped fresh parsley
100 ml (3½ fl oz) olive oil
100 ml (3½ fl oz) lemon or lime juice
1 tablespoon whole grain mustard
1 tablespoon honey
serves 6-8

i

preparation time
10 minutes

nutritional value per serve
fat: 6.4 g
carbohydrate: 4 g
protein: 1.4 g

1 Separate the cabbage leaves, wash and drain well. Cut the thick vein from each leaf, stack some leaves, form a roll and shred as finely as possible.

2 Halve the spanish onion and slice finely lengthwise. In a bowl, combine cabbage, garlic, chilli, dill, parsley and spanish and green onions.

3 Beat together olive oil, lemon or lime juice, mustard and honey until well blended. Pour over the cabbage and mix well. Chill until ready to serve.

calabrian salad

ingredients

4 medium potatoes, unpeeled
8 firm roma tomatoes
3 spanish onions, sliced thinly
15 small basil leaves
1 heaped teaspoon dried oregano
4 tablespoons olive oil
3 tablespoons white- or
  red-wine vinegar
salt and pepper to taste

serves 6

1 Cover potatoes in cold
  water and boil for 15–20
minutes until just tender.
Drain and leave aside until just
cool enough to handle, then
peel and slice thinly. Place
spanish onions in cold water
and soak for 30 minutes. Drain.

2 Cut tomatoes in half and
  slice. In a bowl, combine
potatoes, tomatoes and
spanish onion.

3 Add basil leaves, oregano,
  olive oil, vinegar and salt
and pepper. Toss carefully and
serve immediately.

i

preparation time
15 minutes

cooking time
20 minutes

**nutritional value
per serve**
fat: 3.8 g
carbohydrate: 5.8 g
protein: 1.5 g

olive oil until well blended. Add whole beets and toss in oil mixture. Wrap each beet in foil and place in a baking pan. Roast for approximately 1 hour until just tender. Peel the beets by sliding off the skin with your fingers then cut into thick slices.

2 Trim tops and bottoms of the fennel bulb and cut in half. Remove a wedge of tough core from each half making a 'v' cut at center. Slice finely lengthwise.

3 Combine the dill, balsamic vinegar, remaining olive oil and salt and pepper to taste.

Beat well until thick. Arrange beets on a serving platter with the thinly sliced fennel and orange. Drizzle over the dill vinaigrette, then scatter the hazelnuts on top.

roasted beet, orange and fennel salad

ingredients

5 large beets
1 tablespoon light brown sugar
1 teaspoon salt
2 tablespoons chopped fresh rosemary
3 tablespoons olive oil
1 bulb fennel
3 blood oranges, segmented
150 g (5 oz) hazelnuts, crushed and toasted

dressing

1 handful dill, chopped
2 tablespoons balsamic vinegar
$\frac{1}{2}$ cup (125 ml, 4 fl oz) olive oil
salt and pepper
serves 4-6

1 Preheat the oven to 180°C (350°F, gas mark 4). Wash and trim the beets at root and stem ends leaving $\frac{1}{2}$ inch of root and stem but do not peel. In a small bowl, combine light brown sugar, 1 teaspoon salt, rosemary and 3 tablespoons

i

preparation time
20 minutes

cooking time
1 hour

nutritional value per serve
fat: 5.8 g
carbohydrate: 7.8 g
protein: 2.6 g

green bean salad

preparation time
25 minutes, plus
2 hours
refrigeration

**nutritional value
per serve**
fat: 8.4 g
carbohydrate: 1.9 g
protein: 2.7 g

ingredients

250 g (8 oz) green beans, trimmed,
    blanched and cooled
250 g (8 oz) fresh white button
    mushrooms
1 red bell pepper, skinned
1/2 spanish onion, sliced
2 tablespoons chopped fresh parsley
1 small mignonette lettuce
4 cherry tomatoes, halved
60 g (2 oz) slivered almonds, toasted
dressing
4 tablespoons olive oil
2 tablespoons tarragon vinegar
2 teaspoons dijon mustard
1/2 teaspoon salt
1/2 teaspoon cracked black pepper
serves 4

1 Place beans into a pan of boiling water and cook uncovered for 4–5 minutes until just tender. Drain immediately, refresh in ice cold water. Drain and dry completely on a clean kitchen cloth.

2 Wipe over the mushrooms with damp paper towels and slice thinly. Cut the skinned bell pepper into thin strips. In a bowl, lightly toss beans, mushrooms, bell pepper, onion and parsley. In a small bowl, combine oil, vinegar, mustard, salt and

pepper, and toss through the salad. Refrigerate for 2 hours.

3 Line a platter with lettuce leaves. Arrange salad on top, garnish with tomato quarters and sprinkle over toasted almonds.

kiwifruit and watercress salad

ingredients

¹/₂ bunch watercress, washed drained and dried
3 kiwifruit
125 g (4 oz) small white button mushrooms
75 g (2¹/₂ oz) drained sun-dried tomatoes, packed in oil

dressing

2 tablespoons virgin olive oil
1 tablespoon red-wine vinegar
¹/₂ teaspoon salt
freshly ground black pepper

serves 4

1 Pluck the sprigs from the watercress discarding the coarse stems. Peel and slice the kiwifruit. Place sprigs and kiwifruit into a large bowl.

2 Wipe mushrooms over damp paper towels and trim the ends of the stems. Slice thinly and add to the bowl. Cut the sun-dried tomatoes in half, add to the bowl and toss lightly to distribute the ingredients.

3 In a pitcher, beat together oil, vinegar, salt and pepper. Drizzle over the salad in a thin stream and toss gently. Divide between 4 salad plates and serve immediately.

i

preparation time
15 minutes

nutritional value per serve
fat: 7.9 g
carbohydrate: 6.8 g
protein: 2.4 g

crisp celery salad

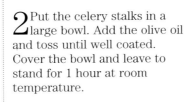

ingredients

1 bunch celery
5 tablespoons extra virgin olive oil
2 tablespoons white-wine vinegar
1 teaspoon dijon mustard
salt and freshly ground black pepper
serves 6

1 Trim the celery and cut each stalk into 2¹/₂ inch pieces; wash and drain. Cut each piece into ¹/₄ inch wide matchsticks. Plunge the celery stalks into a saucepan of boiling water for 30 seconds, drain immediately and place into a bowl of iced water for 1 minute. Drain well.

2 Put the celery stalks in a large bowl. Add the olive oil and toss until well coated. Cover the bowl and leave to stand for 1 hour at room temperature.

3 In a salad bowl, beat the vinegar and mustard together. Add salt and pepper to taste. Add celery and olive oil to the salad bowl and toss well. Serve at once.

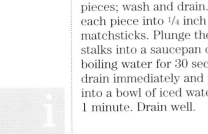

preparation time
15 minutes, plus
1 hour standing

cooking time
1 minute

**nutritional value
per serve**
fat: 19.8 g
carbohydrate: 1.7 g
protein: 0.5 g

tomato salad napolitano

ingredients

6 large ripe tomatoes, each
  cut into 8 wedges
1 spanish onion, thinly sliced
185 g (6 oz) pecorino cheese,
  coarsely grated
2 teaspoons shredded fresh basil
1 teaspoon chopped fresh oregano
vinaigrette
⅓ cup (90 ml, 3 fl oz) olive oil
4 tablespoons white-wine vinegar
½ teaspoon sugar
½ teaspoon salt
¼ teaspoon pepper
serves 6

1 In a large bowl, combine tomato wedges and onion slices. Add the cheese and mix well.

2 In a small bowl, beat together olive oil, white-wine vinegar, sugar, salt and pepper. In another bowl, place the basil and oregano. Mix in the vinaigrette. Pour over the tomato mixture and toss well. Serve at room temperature.

i

preparation time
10 minutes

**nutritional value
per serve**
fat: 8.3 g
carbohydrate: 1.9 g
protein: 4.2 g

tortilla salad mexicana

ingredients

salad
oil for frying
4 corn tortillas, cut into 1/4 inch wide
   strips
225 g (7 1/2 oz) green cabbage,
   finely shredded
135 g (4 1/2 oz) iceberg lettuce,
finely shredded
1 mango, peeled and diced
155 g (5 oz) jîcama or swede,
   peeled and diced
1 spanish onion, finely diced
3 red bell peppers, roasted, peeled
   and sliced
80 g (2 3/4 oz) pumpkin seeds,
   shelled and toasted
1/2 bunch cilantro, chopped
salt and black pepper

dressing
1 small mango, peeled, and flesh diced
1/2 cup (125 ml, 4 fl oz) grapefruit juice
4 tablespoons fresh lime juice
1-2 small red chilli peppers, deseeded
4 green onions, chopped
2 tablespoons vegetable oil
1 clove garlic

serves 4

1 Place 1 mango, grapefruit and lime juice, chilli peppers, green onions, garlic and 2 tablespoons of oil in a blender or food processor and blend until smooth. Set aside.

2 Heat oil in heavy-bottomed medium-sized saucepan over medium-high heat. Add a handful of tortilla strips and cook about 4 minutes until crisp, then remove from the oil and drain on absorbent paper. Repeat with remainder.

3 Combine cabbage, lettuce, mango, jîcama or swede, onion, bell peppers, pumpkin seeds and cilantro in a large bowl. Toss with enough dressing to coat, adding salt and black pepper to taste. Top with the fried tortilla and serve.

preparation time
10 minutes

cooking time
6 minutes

nutritional value per serve
fat: 4.8 g
carbohydrate: 7.1 g
protein: 2.2 g

asian gingered coleslaw

ingredients

coleslaw

¹/₂ large savoy cabbage, finely sliced
4 baby bok choy (pak choi), leaves
   separated and sliced
8 green onions, julienned lengthways
200 g (7 oz) can sliced water
   chestnuts, drained
2 medium carrots, finely julienned
2 stalks lemon grass, finely sliced
4 kaffir lime leaves, finely sliced
1 bunch cilantro, roughly chopped
90 g (3 oz) peanuts or sunflower seeds,
   crushed and toasted

dressing

2 tablespoons mayonnaise
2 tablespoons yogurt
juice of 2 lemons
juice of 1 lime
1 tablespoon grated fresh ginger
4 tablespoons rice vinegar
salt and black pepper

serves 6

i

preparation time
20 minutes

**nutritional value
per serve**
fat: 2.4 g
carbohydrate: 3.3 g
protein: 2.3 g

1 In a large bowl, combine cabbage, bok choy, green onions, water chestnuts, carrots, lemon grass and lime leaves. Toss thoroughly.

2 In a pitcher, beat together mayonnaise, yogurt, lemon and lime juice, ginger, vinegar, salt and pepper until smooth. Pour over salad ingredients and toss thoroughly. Mix through cilantro and sprinkle with peanuts or sunflower seeds.

bell pepper salad

ingredients

2 red bell peppers, quartered
1 yellow bell pepper, quartered
1 green bell pepper, quartered
3 tablespoons olive oil
3 tablespoons lemon juice
1 clove garlic, chopped
60 g (2 oz) mixed herbs such as parsley, oregano, chives, basil, chopped
serves 4-6

preparation time
15 minutes

cooking time
10 minutes

nutritional value per serve
fat: 10.1 g
carbohydrate: 2.6 g
protein: 1.4 g

1 Trim the top and bottom of each bell pepper and cut into quarters making 4 flat pieces. Trim off any inside veins and rub skin side with oil. Place skin side up, under a preheated hot broiler and cook until skins are blistered. Place in a plastic bag and set aside until cool enough to handle. Peel off skins.

2 Cut each quarter into three or four strips and place in a serving dish. Add oil, lemon juice, garlic and herbs to taste. Toss to coat. Serve at room temperature.

spinach grapefruit salad

ingredients

1 bunch fresh young spinach leaves,
   rinsed and dried, leaves torn into pieces
1 large grapefruit, segmented
$^{1}/_{2}$ spanish onion, diced
$^{1}/_{2}$ small red cabbage, shredded
3 tablespoons olive oil
2 tablespoons red-wine vinegar
3 tablespoons orange juice
salt and pepper to taste
zest of 1 orange, cut into strips
serves 4

i

preparation time
10 minutes

**nutritional value
per serve**
fat: 4.8 g
carbohydrate: 3.0 g
protein: 1.6 g

1 In a salad bowl, place spinach, grapefruit, onion and cabbage. Toss well.

2 In a small bowl, beat together oil, vinegar, orange juice and salt and pepper. Pour over the salad and toss lightly. Serve at once, garnished with thin strips of orange zest.

hot brussel sprouts salad with horseradish sauce

ingredients

750 g (1½ lb) brussel sprouts
3 large carrots, peeled
3 leeks, trimmed
2 tablespoons butter
3 teaspoons horseradish cream
3 tablespoons cider vinegar
1 tablespoon finely chopped parsley
½ teaspoon salt
ground black pepper
serves 6-8

i

preparation time
10 minutes

cooking time
12 minutes

**nutritional value
per serve**
fat: 2.7 g
carbohydrate: 3.1 g
protein: 2.7 g

1 Trim outer leaves and stem end of brussel sprouts. Cut carrots into 1 inch slices and leeks into ½ inch pieces. Steam brussel sprouts, carrots and leeks for 10–12 minutes until tender and then drain.

2 Melt butter in a pan. Stir in vinegar, horseradish, parsley, and salt and pepper to taste. Heat until bubbling. Toss well with hot vegetables and serve immediately.

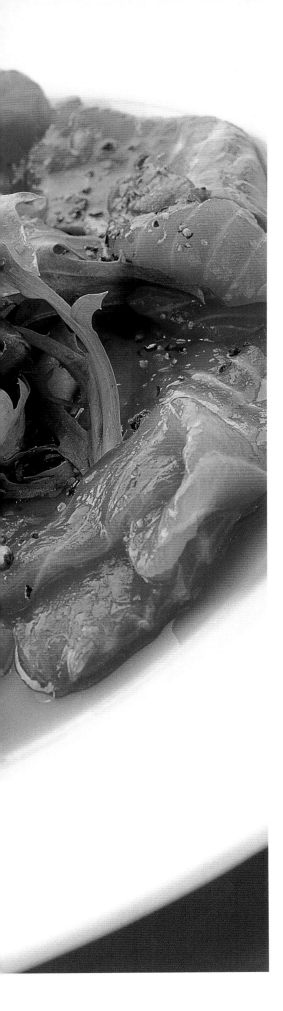

buffet

marinated chicken and pear salad

ingredients

1 large cooked chicken, chopped
   into $^1/_2$ inch-wide strips
200 g (7 oz) dried pear halves,
   halved again

salad
1 coral lettuce
1 mignonette lettuce
1 bunch rocket
2 lebanese cucumbers, thinly sliced
1 small spanish onion, thinly sliced
1 tablespoon olive oil

marinade
$^1/_2$ cup (125 ml, 4 fl oz) olive oil
$^1/_2$ cup (125 ml, 4 fl oz) orange juice
40 g ($1^1/_4$ oz) seeded raisins
2 tablespoons red-wine vinegar
3 whole cloves
2 tablespoons pine nuts
$^1/_2$ teaspoon finely chopped red chilli
   pepper
salt and pepper

serves 12

preparation time
25 minutes,
plus 3 hours
marinating

**nutritional value
per serve**
fat: 9.6 g
carbohydrate: 7.1 g
protein: 6.6 g

1 In a flat-bottomed container, place chicken and top with pears.

2 In a bowl, combine orange juice, raisins, vinegar, cloves, pine nuts, red chilli pepper, $^1/_2$ cup olive oil, and salt and pepper to taste. Pour over the chicken. Cover and refrigerate at least 3 hours. Turn chicken and pears after $1^1/_2$ hours so top pieces sit in the marinade. Wrap washed lettuce leaves and rocket in a damp cloth and refrigerate to crisp.

3 Place salad leaves on a platter and arrange over the chicken, pears, cucumber and onions. Spoon over pine nuts and raisins from the marinade. Beat the remaining marinade again with the extra oil and drizzle over the salad.

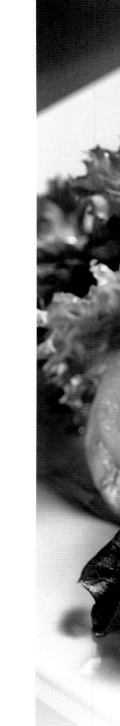

pasta salad with sugar snap peas and salami

ingredients

155 g (5 oz) pasta shells
185 g (6 oz) sugar snap peas, trimmed
125 g (4 oz) italian salami, sliced
  and cut into matchsticks
1 carrot, cut into matchsticks
90 g (3 oz) mozzarella cheese, shredded
vinaigrette
4 tablespoons olive oil
2 tablespoons white-wine vinegar
$1/4$ teaspoon sugar
$1/4$ teaspoon salt
$1/4$ teaspoon pepper
serves 4

i

preparation time
15 minutes

cooking time
12 minutes

**nutritional value
per serve**

fat: 13.1 g
carbohydrate: 18.7 g
protein: 10.6 g

1 Cook pasta shells in a pan of boiling water for about 12 minutes until al dente. Drain, rinse under cold running water and drain again.

2 Plunge sugar snap peas into a pan of boiling water. Bring back to the boil and cook for 30 seconds. Drain immediately and plunge into a bowl of iced water for 2 minutes. Drain and pat dry with paper towels.

3 In a salad bowl, combine pasta shells, sugar snap peas, salami, carrot and mozzarella. In a small bowl, combine olive oil, white-wine vinegar, sugar, salt and pepper. Drizzle vinaigrette over pasta and toss well. Serve lightly chilled.

lobster pineapple salad

ingredients

1 ripe pineapple with the top on
500 g (1 lb) cooked lobster meat
500 g (1 lb) cooked fish fillets
3 stalks celery, chopped
115 g (4oz) blanched almonds, chopped
$^2/_3$ (170ml, $5^1/_2$fl oz) cup mayonnaise
1 teaspoon curry powder
$^1/_2$ cup (125ml, 4 fl oz) plain yogurt

serves 6-8

preparation time
30 minutes,
plus 2 hours
refrigeration

**nutritional value
per serve**
fat: 7.3 g
carbohydrate: 4.2 g
protein: 10.6 g

1 Cut the pineapple lengthwise through the leaves and down to the base. Cut out the pineapple flesh, cut into chunks removing any core. Scrape inside of shell reserving any juice. Set shells aside for serving.

2 Cut the lobster meat into dice and break the fish fillets into bite-sized pieces. Combine lobster, reserved pineapple juice and fish pieces. Cover and refrigerate for 2 hours.

3 Mix the celery, almonds and pineapple chunks together. Add the lobster and fish pieces. Mix mayonnaise, curry powder and yogurt together and carefully toss through the salad. Pile into the pineapple shells.

japanese marinated salmon, cucumber and daikon salad

ingredients

700 g (1 lb 7 oz) fillet salmon, center cut
6 tablespoons mirin
3 tablespoons soy sauce
1 tablespoon grated fresh ginger
1 teaspoon sesame oil
1 continental cucumber, washed
1 teaspoon sea salt
1 tablespoon superfine sugar
3 tablespoons rice vinegar
1 endive (curly chicory)
1 daikon (japanese white radish),
 finely julienned

serves 6-8

2 Beat together mirin, soy, ginger and sesame oil then remove 2 tablespoons and reserve. Pour the remainder over the sliced salmon and cover with plastic wrap. Place in the refrigerator to marinate for 2 hours.

3 Using a potato peeler or food slicer cut the cucumber into long, thin ribbons from each side avoiding the seeds. Break chicory into bite-sized pieces and in a large bowl toss together with cucumber and daikon. Mix together the sea salt, sugar and rice vinegar and toss through the salad.

4 Pile the endive salad into the center of individual appetizer plates or a large platter and arrange the marinated salmon around the edge. Drizzle reserved mirin over the salad.

1 Using an extremely sharp knife, slice the salmon very thinly placing the knife at an angle. Place the slices neatly in a flat-bottomed dish.

i

preparation time
30 minutes,
plus 2 hours
marinating

**nutritional value
per serve**
fat: 3.4 g
carbohydrate: 1.8 g
protein: 8.8 g

asparagus and baby green beans with hazelnut dressing

ingredients

dressing

4 tablespoons lemon juice
4 tablespoons white-wine vinegar
3 egg yolks
1 cup (250 ml, 8 fl oz) hazelnut oil
2 tablespoons chopped dill
160 g (5 ½ oz) toasted hazelnuts, chopped
6 bunches asparagus, trimmed
1 kg (2 lb) baby green beans, topped and tailed
2 red bell peppers, finely julienned

serves 15

i

preparation time
15 minutes

cooking time
2 minutes

nutritional value
fat: 12.5 g
carbohydrate: 2 g
protein: 2.9 g

1 Blend lemon juice, vinegar and egg yolks in a food processor until pale and creamy. Slowly drizzle in oil until the dressing comes together. Remove from processor and stir in dill and toasted nuts. Season to taste.

2 Bring a large pan of water to the boil. Add asparagus and beans and simmer for 1–2 minutes until just tender. Drain immediately and refresh in cold water, drain well. Arrange asparagus, beans and bell pepper strips on a large platter in layers, drizzling each layer with dressing.

shrimp and grape salad

ingredients

1kg (2 lb) cooked shrimp
1 cup (250 ml, 8 fl oz) sour cream
1 cup (250 g, 8 oz) mayonnaise
juice of 1 small lemon
$1/4$ teaspoon tabasco sauce
2 cups white grapes, washed, dried
    and stems removed
2 tablespoons chopped fresh dill
2 tablespoons chopped fresh chives
freshly ground black pepper to taste
serves 4

preparation time
10 minutes,
plus 4 hours
refrigeration

nutritional value
fat: 8 .1 g
carbohydrate: 5 g
protein: 12.1 g

1 Shell and devein the shrimp. Beat the sour cream, mayonnaise, lemon juice and tabasco together.

2 Put prepared shrimp into a serving bowl. Pour over dressing and toss gently. Add the grapes and toss again. Sprinkle on chopped dill and chives and pepper. Toss once more and refrigerate covered, for at least 4 hours.

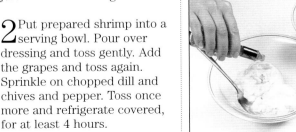

sweet potato and peanut salad

ingredients

2 kg (4 lb) sweet potato, peeled
6 tablespoons olive oil
20 cloves garlic, unpeeled
salt and pepper
1 spanish onion, finely chopped
1-2 small red chilli peppers,
 finely chopped
2 handfuls fresh herbs of your choice
2 tablespoons balsamic vinegar
320 g (11 oz) roasted peanuts
salt and freshly ground pepper
serves 10-12

i

preparation time
15 minutes

cooking time
40 minutes

nutritional value
fat: 9.4 g
carbohydrate: 12.2 g
protein: 4.3 g

1 Peel and cut the sweet potato into large chunks. Toss with 2 tablespoons of the olive oil and place in a large baking pan with the garlic cloves. Season to taste with salt and pepper and bake at 220°C (425°F, gas mark 7) for about 40 minutes or until the sweet potato is tender and golden around the edges. Remove from the oven.

2 Place cooked sweet potato on a platter, mix the spanish onion, chilli pepper, fresh herbs together and sprinkle over the sweet potato.

3 Beat the remaining 4 tablespoons olive oil with the salt and pepper and balsamic vinegar, drizzle over the sweet potato. Sprinkle the peanuts over and gently toss the salad. Serve immediately.

thai rice salad

ingredients

3 tablespoons oil
1 tablespoon thai curry paste
1 tablespoon light brown sugar
2 tablespoons lemon juice
4 cups (740 g, 1¹/₂ lb) cooked
   long-grain rice
1 red bell pepper, chopped
6 green onions, chopped
440 g (14 oz) can pineapple pieces,
   drained
1 handful mint, chopped
salt
¹/₄ teaspoon ground black pepper
serves 6

1 Heat 1 tablespoon of oil in a small skillet, add curry paste and fry while stirring for 40 seconds. Remove from heat, add remaining oil, brown sugar, lemon juice and stir well to combine.

2 In a large bowl, place cooked rice and add curry mixture. Toss until mixed through. Add bell pepper, onions, pineapple pieces, mint, salt and pepper. Toss well. Refrigerate until ready to serve.

i

preparation time
10 minutes

cooking time
3 minutes

**nutritional value
per serve**
fat: 4.5 g
carbohydrate: 17.9 g
protein: 1.7 g

thai beef salad with chilli lime dressing

ingredients

500 g (1 lb) beef tenderloin (fillet)
   in one piece
2 cloves garlic, minced
3 tablespoons chopped cilantro
2 tablespoons olive oil
1 tablespoon sweet chilli sauce
2 tablespoons lime juice
2 teaspoons thai fish sauce
2 teaspoons light brown sugar
$\frac{1}{2}$ teaspoon ground cumin
250 g (8 oz) mixed salad leaves,
   washed and crisped
3 tablespoons fresh mint leaves
3 green onions, diagonally sliced
1 red bell pepper, sliced for garnish
serves 4

1 Preheat oven to 220°C (425°F, gas mark 7). Trim off the silvery membrane and brush the fillet with oil. Place in a shallow baking pan and roast in oven for 25 minutes until medium rare. If using a meat thermometer, cook until it reaches 65°C to 70°C (135°F).

2 Remove from oven, cover with foil and rest for 20 minutes. Hold the end firmly with a strip of foil and using a sharp knife, slice very finely.

3 In a bowl, combine garlic, cilantro, oil, chilli sauce, lime juice, fish sauce, sugar and cumin. Arrange salad leaves on a serving platter, drizzle with some of the dressing. Arrange the beef slices on top and pour over remaining dressing. Sprinkle with mint leaves, green onions and bell pepper strips.

i

preparation time
20 minutes

cooking time
25 minutes

**nutritional value
per serve**
fat: 8.5 g
carbohydrate: 1.9 g
protein: 14.7 g

warm caramelized onion and herbed potato salad

ingredients

1.5 kg (3 lb) desiree or pontiac potatoes
2 tablespoons olive oil
4 white onions, sliced
1 handful fresh dill, chopped
1 handful fresh chervil, chopped
1 handful fresh parsley, chopped
zest of 1 lemon
salt and freshly ground black pepper

dressing

$^2/_3$ cup (170 ml, $5^1/_2$ fl oz) olive oil
3 tablespoons white-wine vinegar
juice of 1 lemon
3 cloves garlic

serves 8-10

i

preparation time
10 minutes

cooking time
35 minutes

nutritional value
fat: 10 g
carbohydrate: 9.6 g
protein: 2.4 g

1 Scrub the potatoes to remove all traces of soil and cut into large chunks. Boil in water for 10 minutes until tender but not soft.

2 In a separate pan, heat 2 tablespoons oil and sauté onions over high heat for 2 minutes. Turn heat to low, cover and cook slowly for 20 minutes, stirring occasionally. Uncover, increase heat and stir until a rich caramel color.

3 Drain potatoes and return to pan. In a pitcher, beat white-wine vinegar, lemon juice, garlic and remaining oil until thickened. Pour over hot potatoes and toss. Add dill, parsley, chervil and lemon zest, and salt and freshly ground black pepper to taste. Add the caramelized onions and toss thoroughly. Serve immediately.

tropical shrimp and papaya salad

ingredients

salad
1 iceberg lettuce, washed and crisped
1 radicchio lettuce, washed and crisped
1 large avocado, cut into chunks
1 large grapefruit, segmented
1 papaya, deseeded and cut into chunks
24 medium-sized shrimp, cooked
   and peeled

dressing
5 tablespoons white-wine vinegar
1 egg yolk, beaten
1 clove garlic, minced
$1/2$ cup (125 ml, 4 fl oz) olive oil
1 tablespoon fresh chives,
   finely chopped
salt

serves 4-6

1 In a bowl, beat the vinegar, egg yolk, garlic, oil and chives, and salt to taste until well combined.

2 Mix the lettuces in a large bowl. Add just enough dressing to moisten and toss until lightly coated. Pile in the center of four plates.

3 Arrange the avocado, grapefruit, papaya and shrimp on and around the lettuce. Drizzle with a little dressing and serve the remainder of the dressing separately.

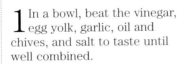

i

preparation time
15 minutes

**nutritional value
per serve**
fat: 8.4 g
carbohydrate: 1.3 g
protein: 2.4 g

glossary

al dente: Italian term to describe pasta and rice that are cooked until tender but still firm to the bite.

bake blind: to bake pastry cases without their fillings. Line the raw pastry case with wax paper and fill with raw rice or dried beans to prevent collapsed sides and puffed base. Remove paper and fill 5 minutes before completion of cooking time.

baste: to spoon hot cooking liquid over food at intervals during cooking to moisten and flavor it.

beat: to make a mixture smooth with rapid and regular motions using a spatula, wire whisk or electric mixer; to make a mixture light and smooth by enclosing air.

beurre manié: equal quantities of butter and flour mixed together to a smooth paste and stirred little by little into a soup, stew or sauce while on the heat to thicken. Stop adding when desired thickness results.

bind: to add egg or a thick sauce to hold ingredients together when cooked.

blanch: to plunge some foods into boiling water for less than a minute and immediately plunge into iced water. This is to brighten the color of some vegetables; to remove skin from tomatoes and nuts.

blend: to mix 2 or more ingredients thoroughly together; do not confuse with blending in an electric blender.

boil: to cook in a liquid brought to boiling point and kept there.

boiling point: when bubbles rise continually and break over the entire surface of the liquid, reaching a temperature of 100°C (212°F). In some cases food is held at this high temperature for a few seconds then heat is turned to low for slower cooking. See simmer.

bouquet garni: a bundle of several herbs tied together with string for easy removal, placed into pots of stock, soups and stews for flavor. A few sprigs of fresh thyme, parsley and bay leaf are used. Can be purchased in sachet form for convenience.

caramelize: to heat sugar in a heavy pan until it liquefies and develops a caramel color. Vegetables such as blanched carrots and sautéed onions may be sprinkled with sugar and caramelized.

chill: to place in the refrigerator or stir over ice until cold.

clarify: to make a liquid clear by removing sediments and impurities. To melt fat and remove any sediment.

coat: to dust or roll food items in flour to cover the surface before the food is cooked. Also, to coat in flour, egg and breadcrumbs.

cool: to stand at room temperature until some or all heat is removed, e.g., cool a little, cool completely.

cream: to make creamy and fluffy by working the mixture with the back of a wooden spoon, usually refers to creaming butter and sugar or margarine. May also be creamed with an electric mixer.

croutons: small cubes of bread, toasted or fried, used as an addition to salads or as a garnish to soups and stews.

crudite: raw vegetable sticks served with a dipping sauce.

crumb: to coat foods in flour, egg and breadcrumbs to form a protective coating for foods that are fried. Also adds flavor, texture and enhances appearance.

cube: to cut into small pieces with six even sides, e.g., cubes of meat.

cut in: to combine fat and flour using 2 knives scissor fashion or with a pastry blender, to make pastry.

deglaze: to dissolve dried out cooking juices left on the bottom and sides of a roasting dish or skillet. Add a little water, wine or stock, scrape and stir over heat until dissolved. Resulting liquid is used to make a flavorsome gravy or added to a sauce or casserole.

degrease: to skim fat from the surface of cooking liquids, e.g., stocks, soups, casseroles.

dice: to cut into small cubes.

dredge: to heavily coat with powdered sugar, sugar, flour or cornstarch.

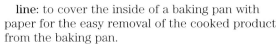

dressing: a mixture added to completed dishes to add moisture and flavor, e.g., salads, cooked vegetables.

drizzle: to pour in a fine thread-like stream moving over a surface.

egg wash: beaten egg with milk or water used to brush over pastry, bread dough or cookies to give a sheen and golden brown color.

essence: a strong flavoring liquid, usually made by distillation. Only a few drops are needed to flavor.

fillet: a piece of prime meat, fish or poultry that is boneless or has all bones removed.

flake: to separate cooked fish into flakes, removing any bones and skin, using 2 forks.

flame: to ignite warmed alcohol over food or to pour into a pan with food, ignite then serve.

flute: to make decorative indentations around the pastry edge before baking.

fold in: combining of a light, whipped or creamed mixture with other ingredients. Add a portion of the other ingredients at a time and mix using a gentle circular motion, over and under the mixture so that air will not be lost. Use a silver spoon or spatula.

glaze: to brush or coat food with a liquid that will give the finished product a glossy appearance, and on baked products, a golden brown color.

grease: to rub the surface of a metal or heatproof dish with oil or fat, to prevent the food from sticking.

herbed butter: softened butter mixed with finely chopped fresh herbs and re-chilled. Used to serve on grilled meats and fish.

hors d'ouvre: small savory foods served as an appetizer, popularly known today as "finger food".

infuse: to steep foods in a liquid until the liquid absorbs their flavor.

joint: to cut poultry and game into serving pieces by dividing at the joint.

julienne: to cut some food, e.g., vegetables and processed meats into fine strips the length of matchsticks. Used for inclusion in salads or as a garnish to cooked dishes.

knead: to work a yeast dough in a pressing, stretching and folding motion with the heel of the hand until smooth and elastic to develop the gluten strands. Non-yeast doughs should be lightly and quickly handled as gluten development is not desired.

line: to cover the inside of a baking pan with paper for the easy removal of the cooked product from the baking pan.

macerate: to stand fruit in a syrup, liqueur or spirit to give added flavor.

marinade: a flavored liquid, into which food is placed for some time to give it flavor and to tenderize. Marinades include an acid ingredient such as vinegar or wine, oil and seasonings.

mask: to evenly cover cooked food portions with a sauce, mayonnaise or savory jelly.

pan-fry: to fry foods in a small amount of fat or oil, sufficient to coat the bottom of the pan.

parboil: to boil until partially cooked. The food is then finished by some other method.

pare: to peel the skin from vegetables and fruit. Peel is the popular term but pare is the name given to the knife used; paring knife.

pith: the white lining between the rind and flesh of oranges, grapefruit and lemons.

pit: to remove stones or seeds from olives, cherries, dates.

pitted: the olives, cherries, dates, etc., with the stone removed, e.g., purchase pitted dates.

poach: to simmer gently in enough hot liquid to almost cover the food so shape will be retained.

pound: to flatten meats with a meat mallet; to reduce to a paste or small particles with a mortar and pestle.

simmer: to cook in liquid just below boiling point at about 96°C (205°F) with small bubbles rising gently to the surface.

skim: to remove fat or froth from the surface of simmering food.

stock: the liquid produced when meat, poultry, fish or vegetables have been simmered in water to extract the flavor. Used as a base for soups, sauces, casseroles, etc. Convenience stock products are available.

sweat: to cook sliced onions or vegetables, in a small amount of butter in a covered pan over low heat, to soften them and release flavor without coloring.

conversions

measurements differ from country to country, so it's important to understand what the differences are. This Measurements Guide gives you simple "at-a-glance" information for using the recipes in this book, wherever you may be.

Cooking is not an exact science – minor variations in measurements won't make a difference to your cooking.

equipment

There is a difference in the size of measuring cups used internationally, but the difference is minimal (only 2–3 teaspoons). We use the Australian standard metric measurements in our recipes:

1 teaspoon ....5 ml   1 tablespoon....20 ml
½ cup......125 ml   1 cup.....250 ml
4 cups...1 liter

Measuring cups come in sets of one cup (250 ml), ½ cup (125 ml), ⅓ cup (80 ml) and ¼ cup (60 ml). Use these for measuring liquids and certain dry ingredients.

Measuring spoons come in a set of four and should be used for measuring dry and liquid ingredients.

When using cup or spoon measures always make them level (unless the recipe indicates otherwise).

dry versus wet ingredients

While this system of measures is consistent for liquids, it's more difficult to quantify dry ingredients. For instance, one level cup equals: 200 g of brown sugar; 210 g of superfine sugar; and 110 g of powdered sugar.

When measuring dry ingredients such as flour, don't push the flour down or shake it into the cup. It is best just to spoon the flour in until it reaches the desired amount. When measuring liquids use a clear vessel indicating metric levels.

Always use medium eggs (1.5-2.5 oz) when eggs are required in a recipe.

dry

metric (grams)	imperial (ounces)
30 g	1 oz
60 g	2 oz
90 g	3 oz
100 g	3½ oz
125 g	4 oz
150 g	5 oz
185 g	6 oz
200 g	7 oz
250 g	8 oz
280 g	9 oz
315 g	10 oz
330 g	11 oz
370 g	12 oz
400 g	13 oz
440 g	14 oz
470 g	15 oz
500 g	16 oz (1 lb)
750 g	24 oz (1½ lb)
1000 g (1 kg)	32 oz (2 lb)

liquids

metric (milliliters)	imperial (fluid ounces)
30 ml	1 fl oz
60 ml	2 fl oz
90 ml	3 fl oz
100 ml	3½ fl oz
125 ml	4 fl oz
150 ml	5 fl oz
190 ml	6 fl oz
250 ml	8 fl oz
300 ml	10 fl oz
500 ml	16 fl oz
600 ml	20 fl oz (1 pint)*
1000 ml (1 liter)	32 fl oz

*Note: an American pint is 16 fl oz.

oven
Your oven should always be at the right temperature before placing the food in it to be cooked. Note that if your oven doesn't have a fan you may need to cook food for a little longer.

microwave
It is difficult to give an exact cooking time for microwave cooking. It is best to watch what you are cooking closely to monitor its progress.

standing time
Many foods continue to cook when you take them out of the oven or microwave. If a recipe states that the food needs to "stand" after cooking, be sure not to overcook the dish.

can sizes
The can sizes available in your supermarket or grocery store may not be the same as specified in the recipe. Don't worry if there is a small variation in size—it's unlikely to make a difference to the end result.

cooking temperatures	°C (celsius)	°F (fahrenheit)	gas mark
very slow	120	250	1/2
slow	150	300	2
moderately slow	160	315	2-3
moderate	180	350	4
moderate hot	190	375	5
	200	400	6
hot	220	425	7
very hot	230	450	8
	240	475	9
	250	500	10

index